The Feasts of Israel for Christians

A Brief Overview of Israel's Festivals in the Hebrew Scriptures and Their Relevance to Christianity

Eitan Bar

Copyright © 2023 by Eitan Bar

ISBN: 9798856195445

All rights reserved.

No portion of this book may be reproduced in any form without written permission from the publisher or author, except as permitted by U.S. copyright law.

Contents

1. Introduction   1
2. A Brief Overview of Jewish Festivals   3
3. Passover   6
4. The Festival of Unleavened Bread   11
5. The Festival of First Fruits   14
6. The Feast of Weeks or Pentecost   18
7. The Feast of Trumpets   21
8. The Day of Atonement   24
9. The Feast of Tabernacles   28
10. Other Important Jewish Observances for Christians   32
11. The Sabbath   35
12. Embracing Jewish Festivals as a Christian Community   39

Introduction

The purpose of this book is to serve as a guide to the Christian community in understanding and celebrating the major Jewish festivals described in the Old Testament of the Bible.

While Christianity has roots in Judaism and shares the same Biblical history as the Old Testament, it is common for Christians to overlook the importance and relevance of Jewish festivals in their faith journey. This book is a humble attempt to bridge this gap and help Christians delve into these rich traditions with profound biblical and theological significance.

Understanding the Shared Heritage of Judaism and Christianity is crucial for gaining a deeper understanding of the Christian faith and Jesus' teachings. The Old Testament, which forms the religious scripture of Judaism, is also the first part of the Christian Bible. Therefore, the religious observances, laws, prophecies, and historical accounts within it are also integral to Christianity.

Jesus himself was a Jew and participated in these Jewish festivals, and the New Testament provides several accounts of this. By understanding these festivals and their biblical context, Christians can gain new perspectives on Jesus' teachings and their own faith.

The Biblical Basis for Understanding Jewish Festivals will be outlined throughout this book. Each festival will be explored, delving into the biblical basis for the festival, its symbolism and meaning in the Jewish faith, and how it was observed in biblical times. We will then explore how Christians can celebrate and understand each festival in the context of their faith.

The Jewish festivals are more than mere historical or cultural observances. They are profound spiritual practices that carry deep symbolism and prophetic significance. For Christians, understanding these festivals can provide a richer, deeper understanding of Jesus' life, teachings, and His fulfillment of biblical prophecies.

Our journey will take us from Passover, the feast commemorating the Exodus from Egypt, through to the joyful observance of the Feast of Tabernacles, with each festival shedding a unique light on biblical teachings and their resonance in Christianity.

This exploration is not meant to blur the lines between the two faiths or imply that they are the same. Rather, it is to celebrate the shared heritage, foster greater interfaith understanding, and deepen our spiritual perspectives. I invite you to join me on this enlightening journey through the Jewish festivals as we explore their biblical roots, their significance, and the beautiful ways they can enhance our Christian faith.

A Brief Overview of Jewish Festivals

As we set forth on this enlightening journey, it's crucial first to establish a comprehensive understanding of Jewish festivals' nature and their profound significance within the scriptures of the Bible. Often denoted as the 'Feasts of the Lord,' Jewish festivals are special observances, mandates that God Himself commanded in the Old Testament. These festivals play a multifaceted role within the tapestry of the Jewish faith. They serve as pivotal reminders of historical events that shaped the course of Israel's history, act as profound expressions of gratitude to God, and prophetically point to the Messiah's advent and mission—a prophecy that forms a cornerstone of Christian belief.

To fully comprehend the importance of Jewish festivals, we must grasp their position as integral parts of the Bible, within both historical and theological contexts. The detailed instructions for these festivals, given directly by God to the Israelites, find their place in the sacred books of Exodus, Leviticus, Numbers, and Deuteronomy. These festivals carry weighty historical, spiritual, and prophetic meanings. Each festival forms a link that connects the Israelites, and by extension, Christians, to defining moments in religious history. These festivals offer invaluable opportunities for worship, thanksgiving, and reflection on future events, many of which Christians believe find their fulfillment in the life and mission of Jesus Christ.

The Bible meticulously outlines seven major festivals: Passover (Pesach), the Feast of Unleavened Bread (Chag HaMatzot), the Feast of First Fruits (Bikkurim), the Feast of Weeks or Pentecost (Shavuot), the Feast of Trumpets (Rosh Hashanah), the Day of Atonement (Yom Kippur), and the Feast of Tabernacles (Sukkot). Spread across the Jewish religious calendar year, each festival possesses a unique spiritual significance that we will dissect and explore in the forthcoming chapters.

One pivotal element in understanding the Jewish festivals is grasping the nature of the Jewish calendar itself. This calendar is based on lunar cycles, unlike the solar-based Gregorian calendar commonly used today. This distinction results in the Jewish festivals falling on different dates of the Gregorian calendar each year. A solid understanding of this calendar is key to celebrating the festivals at their prescribed times, enabling a deeper, more meaningful engagement with these observances.

Now that we have laid the necessary foundation, I invite you to embark on this journey as we delve into each festival in detail, commencing with the first significant festival on the Jewish calendar - Passover. As we dive deep into each festival, we aim to unravel their biblical origins, the historical contexts that shaped them, their spiritual resonance across time, and their enduring significance today. Moreover, we'll explore how modern-day Christians can engage with these age-old observances in ways that enrich their understanding of their faith, build a bridge to their spiritual heritage, and open a window into the deep historical and spiritual bonds that link Christianity and Judaism. Let us set forth, then, on this path of discovery, enlightenment, and spiritual enrichment.

Passover

(Pesach)

Marking one of the seminal events in the history of the Jewish people, Passover, or Pesach in Hebrew, stands as one of the most significant Jewish festivals. It is the narrative heartbeat of the Exodus story, an account fraught with profound theological and spiritual connotations that resonate through Jewish and Christian traditions alike.

To fully appreciate the importance of Passover, we must trace its origin back to the scriptural records in Exodus 12. Here, the chronicle of a miraculous deliverance unfolds a momentous episode when God intervened to liberate the Israelites from the yoke of Egyptian bondage.

The Israelites received specific instructions: each family was to slaughter a lamb, referred to as the Paschal Lamb, and apply its blood to the doorposts and lintel of their homes. This sign, the blood of the lamb, served as a divine marker. When the Angel of Death descended upon Egypt to enact the final and most devastating plague, the death of every firstborn, he would 'pass over' any household marked with the lamb's blood. This event, the passing over of the Angel of Death, thus gives the festival its name - Passover.

This miraculous sparing of the Israelites precipitated the climax of the ten plagues narrative, leading to Pharaoh's final capitulation and the subsequent liberation of the Israelites, marking the beginning of their exodus from Egypt.

Passover, at its core, is a festival that celebrates deliverance and freedom. It commemorates the extraordinary event of the Israelites' liberation from centuries of oppression and slavery under Egyptian rule. Simultaneously, Passover serves as a potent testament to God's sovereignty, justice, and mercy, showcasing His ability and willingness to intervene on behalf of His people.

Furthermore, from a Christian perspective, Passover foreshadows humanity's ultimate redemption through the sacrifice of Jesus Christ, often referred to as the 'Lamb of God.' This Christian interpretation views Jesus as the ultimate Passover lamb, a sacrifice whose blood brings deliverance from spiritual bondage, just as the original Paschal Lamb's blood led to the physical liberation of the Israelites from Egypt.

While Passover isn't typically incorporated into the Christian liturgical calendar, Christians can nonetheless take part in its commemoration, using it as a powerful tool to deepen their understanding of their faith's salvation history. This understanding isn't simply a theoretical or theological one but can be deeply experiential, bringing the narratives of the Bible to life in fresh and enlightening ways.

One way to do this is through participating in, or at least closely observing a Seder meal. The Seder meal is a rich, multi-sensory ceremonial feast that marks the beginning of the Passover. It's filled with symbolism and ritual, and each element tells a part of the Passover story.

For example, consider the Passover lamb, a central part of the meal. In the original Passover event, the blood of this lamb was used to mark the doorposts of the Israelites' houses, protecting them from the last and most devastating of the plagues God sent to Egypt. In Christian interpretation, this lamb prefigures Jesus, often referred to as the "Lamb of God." Just as the Passover lamb's blood saved the Israelites from physical death, Christians believe Jesus' sacrificial death and resurrection offer spiritual salvation to all of humanity.

The unleavened bread, or MATZAH, consumed during the Seder, is another powerful symbol. In the hurried flight from Egypt, the Israelites didn't have time to wait for their bread to rise. In the Christian context, this bread is seen to represent the sinless nature of Jesus. In the Last Supper, Jesus broke bread and declared it to be His body, given for His followers. The use of unleavened bread in this context deepens the connection between the Seder meal and Christian communion practices.

Lastly, the bitter herbs, or MAROR, serve to remind participants of the bitterness of slavery the Israelites suffered in Egypt. For Christians, this can symbolize the bitter suffering Jesus endured on the cross, as well as the hardships we might face in our own spiritual journeys.

By engaging with these symbols, Christians can find a deeper understanding of how the Old Testament narratives and rituals are seen to prefigure the events of the New Testament. Participating in a Seder can offer Christians a powerful, tangible connection to their faith's Jewish roots, enriching their understanding of key Christian doctrines and practices.

The Last Supper, which Jesus shared with His disciples before His crucifixion, was essentially a Passover meal. During this meal, Jesus initiated what traditional churches would consider the sacrament of the Eucharist, more widely known as Communion. He used the unleavened bread to symbolize His body, soon to be broken, and the wine as His blood, soon to be shed. In doing so, Jesus imbued the symbols of the Passover with new layers of meaning, establishing a link between this ancient Jewish observance and a key Christian sacrament.

Therefore, remembering and understanding Passover can significantly deepen Christians' appreciation for the Eucharist or Communion sacrament. It provides a more profound understanding of Jesus Christ's role as the sacrificial lamb who takes away the sins of the world, establishing a bridge between the Old Testament's narrative of physical liberation and the New Testament's message of spiritual salvation.

In Jesus

In the New Testament, the Gospels recount Jesus sharing the Passover meal, known as "the Last Supper," with his disciples just before his arrest and crucifixion (Matthew 26:17-30, Mark 14:12-26, Luke 22:7-23). This was not just any Passover meal; it was one imbued with new significance. As they broke bread and drank wine, Jesus introduced powerful symbols that would define Christian worship for millennia. The unleavened bread, always a reminder of the Israelites' swift departure from Egypt, was now emblematic of Jesus' body, broken for many. The wine, traditionally a symbol of joy and God's blessings, took on a deeper significance as Jesus likened it to his blood, poured out for the forgiveness of sins.

Furthermore, the timing of Jesus' crucifixion during the Passover festival is not just coincidental; it's deeply symbolic. In John 1:29, John the Baptist declares upon seeing Jesus, "Behold, the Lamb of God, who takes away the sin of the world!" Jesus is repeatedly likened to the Passover lamb, a perfect and blameless sacrifice. His death, much like the lamb's sacrifice, becomes the means of deliverance, not from physical bondage as in Egypt, but from the spiritual bondage of sin.

For many Christians, the Eucharist or Communion isn't just a ritual; it's a powerful reminder of the lengths to which God went to save humanity. Every time believers partake in this, they're not only connecting with the sacrifice of Jesus but also with the broader story of redemption that spans both Testaments.

In conclusion, Passover, while primarily a Jewish festival, offers profound insights for Christians. The stories of deliverance, sacrifice, and hope resonate deeply with the Christian narrative. As we remember the Exodus and Jesus' sacrifice, we're reminded that God's love and commitment to redemption are unchanging, stretching across generations and bridging entire testaments. The Passover lamb and the Lamb of God converge in a story of unparalleled grace, urging believers of all generations to remember, reflect, and rejoice.

As we leave the discussion on Passover, we transition to the Feast of Unleavened Bread. This feast begins immediately after Passover, extending the period of remembrance and carrying its own unique historical, symbolic, and theological significance within both Jewish and Christian traditions.

The Festival of Unleavened Bread

(Chag HaMatzot)

Closely intertwined with Passover in both timing and thematic resonance, the Feast of Unleavened Bread, or Chag HaMatzot in Hebrew, is another significant Jewish festival. This seven-day festival begins immediately on the heels of Passover, so much so that the two are often combined or confused. However, the Festival of Unleavened Bread carries its own unique, symbolic, and historical significance.

The foundation for the Festival of Unleavened Bread is established in Exodus 12:14-20, where, in the narrative's aftermath of the Passover, the Israelites received instructions to remove all leaven from their houses. For seven days, they were to eat only unleavened bread, known as matzah. This practice served to recall the haste with which they departed from Egypt, a rushed escape that left no time for the usual preparation and leavening of bread.

This quick exodus, encapsulated in the unrisen bread, became a physical, tangible memory for the Israelites, a reminder of their sudden liberation and the abrupt shift from a life of oppression to a journey towards freedom.

Within the biblical context, leaven often serves as a metaphor for sin or moral corruption. The act of removing all leaven from the house, then, becomes a symbolic act of purging sin and spiritual impurity from one's life. Thus, the Festival of Unleavened Bread serves not just as a historical commemoration but also as a time for introspection, self-examination, and spiritual purification

During this week-long period, the Jewish people are reminded of their ancestors' hasty departure from Egypt, but more importantly, they engage in a deliberate, ritualistic removal of 'sin,' symbolized by the leaven. This time serves as an opportunity to reflect on personal shortcomings, seek forgiveness, and renew commitments to live according to God's laws.

In the context of the Last Supper, Jesus employed the symbolism of unleavened bread to represent His body, which was about to be broken for the redemption of humanity's sins. In this way, the Festival of Unleavened Bread's themes find resonance in the Christian understanding of Christ's sacrifice and redemption.

Understanding this festival, its roots, and its symbolism can provide Christians with a more profound appreciation of Christ's atoning work and the significance of the bread used in the Communion service. It offers an opportunity to engage in meaningful self-examination, to confess and 'remove' sins, and to renew commitment to living a Christ-like life.

In Jesus

During the Festival of Unleavened Bread, it's profound to reflect on Jesus' declaration: "I am the bread of life. Whoever comes to me will never go hungry, and whoever believes in me will never be thirsty" (John 6:35). In calling Himself the bread of life, Jesus offers Himself as the sustenance that truly satisfies, free from the "leaven" of sin, unbelief, and insincerity.

For Christians, the Festival of Unleavened Bread can serve as a time of spiritual reflection, confession, and renewal. While they may not physically remove leaven from their homes as in the Jewish tradition, the metaphorical process of identifying and 'removing' sin from their lives can be a powerful spiritual exercise.

Paul, in his letter to the Corinthians, draws a direct parallel between Jesus and the unleavened bread. He writes, "For Christ, our Passover lamb, has been sacrificed. Therefore let us keep the Festival, not with the old bread leavened with malice and wickedness, but with the un-leavened bread of sincerity and truth" (1 Corinthians 5:7-8). Here, Paul underscores the purity of Jesus' sacrifice, urging believers to live untainted by the sins of the world, much like the pure, unleavened bread.

As we continue our exploration of Jewish festivals, our journey takes us next to the Feast of First Fruits. This festival, although less known outside of Jewish circles, holds its unique meaning and prophetic significance. It introduces another layer of symbolism and continues the thematic sequence of festivals closely linked to the historical and spiritual narrative of the Israelite journey from liberation to an establishment in the Promised Land.

The Festival of First Fruits

(Bikkurim)

The Festival of First Fruits, 'Bikkurim' in Hebrew, represents an integral celebration in the Jewish religious calendar, marking an early spring festival tied intrinsically to the rhythm of life and the agricultural cycles of the Holy Land. Rooted deeply in both historical and spiritual significance, it provides a lens into the tangible aspects of ancient Israelite life and their interactions with the divine.

The biblical establishment of Bikkurim is delineated in Leviticus 23:9-14. Following the conclusion of the Passover and during the week of the Festival of Unleavened Bread, the Israelites were commanded to bring the first sheaf of their barley harvest to the priest. This sheaf, known as an "OMER," would be waved before the Lord in a ceremonial gesture of offering, a poignant reminder of their dependence on God's providence. This was to be done on the "morrow after the Sabbath" or the first day of the week.

The act of waving the OMER is replete with symbolism. The OMER, being the first sheaf of the barley harvest, represents the first fruits of the Israelites' labor. Waving this OMER before the Lord is a physical manifestation of gratitude, recognizing that the source of their provision is God Himself. Moreover, it's an act of faith, trusting in God's continued providence for the rest of the harvest season.

Beyond the immediate symbolism related to harvest and provision, this ritual also speaks to broader themes of joy, thanksgiving, and dependence on God. The act of waving suggests a movement of joy and celebration, as well as a visible representation of offering something valuable to God.

Bikkurim is a festival centered around the concept of 'firsts.' The act of offering the first sheaf of the barley harvest held dual significance for the Israelites. First, it was an act of gratitude for God's provision. By offering the first and finest of their crops, they acknowledged that everything they had was a blessing from God. Second, it was a display of trust and faith in God's continued blessing and provision throughout the rest of the harvest season.

Moreover, this festival holds deep prophetic significance. In the Christian interpretation, it serves as a foreshadowing of the resurrection of Jesus Christ, marking him as the 'first fruit' of the promise of eternal life.

In Jesus

The Festival of First Fruits, celebrated during the week of Unleavened Bread, beckons Christians to a time of reflection, gratitude, and faith. This festival, deeply rooted in agricultural tradition, saw Israelites bring the first produce of their spring crops to the priest. This gesture was more than just an agricultural act; it symbolized gratitude to God, acknowledging His provision and an expression of trust in the full harvest yet to come.

Paul, in his first letter to the Corinthians, eloquently links Jesus to this festival, describing Him as the "first fruits" of those who have passed away (1 Corinthians 15:20). This depiction isn't mere poetry. The timing of Jesus' resurrection, the day after the Sabbath following Passover, aligns precisely with the Festival of First Fruits. By this divine design, Jesus' resurrection and the festival are forever intertwined, with Christ emerging as the inaugural fruit of the divine harvest, promising resurrection to all believers.

This confluence of events offers a profound realization. Just as the early crops promised a more significant, forthcoming harvest, Jesus' victory over death pledges eternal life and blessings for those who have faith in Him. The resurrection of Christ is not just a singular event but a beacon of hope, hinting at the grander narrative of salvation and redemption.

In contemporary times, the Festival of First Fruits can also serve as a tangible prompt for Christians. It's an occasion to witness God's ongoing provision and an invitation to trust in His future blessings. To commemorate, believers might offer support to local charities, delve into dedicated periods of prayer and thanksgiving, or extend acts of service to their communities. Through these gestures, gratitude and faith become manifest, creating ripples of kindness and generosity.

Understanding the context and significance of the Festival of First Fruits bestows upon Christians a profound appreciation for the resurrection, reinforcing the assurance of their own eternal life. As we journey through the exploration of Jewish festivals, our path leads us to 'Shavuot', or the Feast of Weeks — known as Pentecost in Christian circles. Concluding the spring festivals, this juncture holds immense significance, acting as a bridge between the jubilation of the early harvest and the eager anticipation of the later one.

The Feast of Weeks or Pentecost

(Shavuot)

Stepping into the latter part of the Jewish religious calendar, we encounter the Feast of Weeks, or Shavuot in Hebrew. Known to many Christians as Pentecost, this festival stands apart as the fourth Jewish festival in the religious calendar year. Uniquely, it isn't tied directly to the Exodus narrative that underscores so many other Jewish holidays. Despite this, or perhaps because of it, Shavuot holds its own unique significance in the Jewish faith, embodying historical, theological, and cultural elements that are fundamental to understanding the Jewish tradition.

Unlike the immediate physical liberation remembered in Passover or the swift escape memorialized in the Festival of Unleavened Bread, Shavuot encapsulates a more prolonged, reflective celebration. Found in Leviticus 23:15-22, the Israelites were instructed to count seven full weeks from the Festival of First Fruits before commencing the celebration of Shavuot on the fiftieth day. This festival marked the cessation of the grain harvest season, a time to express gratitude for God's provision and the successful completion of the harvest.

However, Shavuot signifies more than just an agricultural milestone. This festival is also traditionally recognized as commemorating the giving of the Torah to the Israelites at Mount Sinai. According to Jewish tradition, this monumental event transpired precisely seven weeks after the Exodus. Thus, Shavuot not only marks a seasonal transition but also celebrates the receipt of God's law, binding the themes of divine provision and divine guidance into one harmonious event.

In Jesus

For Christians, Pentecost, much like Shavuot for Jews, is a time of celebration and reflection. It's a commemoration of the divine gift of the Holy Spirit, an essential facet of the triune God, and a celebration of the inception of the Church. Understanding the biblical context and significance of Shavuot can thereby enrich Christians' understanding of Pentecost, intertwining the celebration of God's law, His provision, and the Holy Spirit into a profound tapestry of divine love and grace. It's not about a punishment being taken away. It's about a provision given by God.

For Christians, Pentecost, derived from the Greek word for "fiftieth," carries a distinct resonance. Falling fifty days after Jesus' resurrection, it is emblematic of the day when the Holy Spirit descended upon the apostles and other followers of Jesus Christ, as depicted in Acts 2. This profound event, with tongues of fire and the ability to speak in various languages, didn't just fortify the faith of the disciples; it signaled the very birth of the Christian Church.

This transformative experience of the Holy Spirit's descent wasn't just an empowerment for the apostles. It was a fulfillment of Jesus' promise, ensuring that His teachings would not just persist but flourish. This outpouring validated that God's plan, birthed in Jewish tradition, was now expanding, ushering a new covenant for all of humanity.

The juxtaposition of the two commemorations—receiving the Torah and the Holy Spirit's advent—underscores a continuum in God's interaction with humanity. While the Torah provided guidance and a moral code, the Holy Spirit provided the means to internalize and enact these teachings, enabling believers to walk in step with God's heart.

For modern believers, the Feast of Weeks serves as a poignant reminder of two core truths: God's unyielding commitment to guide His people, and the transformative power of His Spirit. It's a call to remember, celebrate, and live out the values imbibed from these divine interventions.

As we transition from the vibrancy of Pentecost and look ahead to the autumnal festivals, our first stop is Rosh Hashanah, the Feast of Trumpets. These later festivals, abundant in prophetic symbolism and cultural nuances, offer Christians an enriching panorama of biblical prophecies, each finding their culmination in the life, sacrifice, and resurrection of Jesus Christ. This exploration is not merely academic; it's a heartfelt journey into the shared heritage of Judaism and Christianity, unveiling the profound interconnectedness of these faiths and their divine orchestrations.

The Feast of Trumpets

(Rosh Hashanah)

Venturing deeper into the tapestry of Jewish festivals, we encounter Rosh Hashanah, also known as the Feast of Trumpets. Signaling the advent of the autumn festivals, Rosh Hashanah rings in the first day of Tishrei, the seventh month in the Jewish calendar. This festival is an invitation into a time of reflection and spiritual renewal, underlined by the stirring sound of the shofar, the ram's horn.

The biblical foundation of Rosh Hashanah is laid out in Leviticus 23:23-25. The Israelites were commanded to set aside their usual work and gather for a sacred assembly marked by the blasts of the trumpet. This was not simply an event of communal bonding but a divine mandate – a call for rest, attentiveness, and collective celebration.

Rosh Hashanah is a festival brimming with symbolism. As the inception of the Jewish civil year, it represents a significant milestone in the passage of time. Traditional Jewish belief upholds Rosh Hashanah as the anniversary of the world's creation and the day when God, with a scribe's precision, inscribes the fate of each individual for the upcoming year in the 'Book of Life'. It is a day steeped in the dichotomy of divine judgment and joyous celebration as it ushers in the new year with introspection, repentance, and hope.

In Jesus

From the Christian vantage point, trumpets carry rich theological undertones that reverberate through the Old to the New Testament. Throughout biblical narratives, trumpets played a multifaceted role: from calling people to assembly, announcing the onset of war, and marking solemn festivals, to symbolizing God's powerful voice and heralding monumental divine interventions.

Diving deeper into the New Testament, the imagery of the trumpet takes on a new layer of eschatological significance. In 1 Thessalonians 4:16, the apostle Paul speaks of the Lord's triumphant return, which will be heralded by "the trumpet call of God." This powerful imagery evokes a sense of anticipation and awe among believers, pointing towards the climactic event of Christ's Second Coming. It's a reminder of the final reunion of the faithful with their Savior.

Moreover, the Feast of Trumpets stands as a symbol of new beginnings. Just as Rosh Hashanah ushers in a fresh start in the Jewish calendar, the New Testament reveals a fresh covenant—eternal and unshakeable—made possible by the sacrificial love of Jesus. By engaging with the Feast of Trumpets, Christians are invited to anticipate anew the promises of God: the final redemption, the realization of God's kingdom on earth, and the everlasting communion with God.

While Christians await the final trumpet call, it is also an opportunity to assess one's spiritual journey. The echoing sound of the shofar should stir the soul, prompting self-reflection, repentance, and a renewed commitment to walk in God's ways. Just as the Jewish tradition uses this day to introspect and turn back to God, Christians can seize this moment to draw closer to Christ, deepening their relationship and fortifying their faith.

The Feast of Trumpets, then, isn't just a historical or cultural observance; it's a powerful reminder of God's continual engagement with humanity and His ultimate plan of redemption. By intertwining the themes of both testaments, believers can better appreciate the intricacies of God's narrative, recognizing the singular return of Christ that binds all prophecies into one harmonious refrain of hope and salvation.

Moving further into the autumnal festivals, we will next delve into the Day of Atonement, known as Yom Kippur. Renowned as the most solemn day in the Jewish calendar, Yom Kippur holds profound significance, particularly within the Christian context. It provides Christians with fresh insights into the understanding of Jesus Christ's atoning sacrifice, offering a unique lens through which to view this critical aspect of Christian belief. When we celebrate these festivals, we continue to uncover the rich connections between Christianity and its Jewish roots, underscoring the profound interplay between these two intertwined faiths.

The Day of Atonement

(Yom Kippur)

As we continue our exploration into Jewish religious festivals, we delve into Yom Kippur, also known as the Day of Atonement. This day is not just another entry in the liturgical calendar; it represents the pinnacle of solemnity for the Jewish community. It is a day dedicated to profound repentance, introspection, and the pursuit of God's forgiveness.

The Book of Leviticus is foundational in the understanding of Yom Kippur (chapters 16 and 23:26-32). The narratives and commandments contained therein outline the rituals and procedures associated with this significant day. The high priest of Israel is instructed to make a sacrifice, first for his own sins and then for those of the people. The rituals culminate with the high priest entering the Holy of Holies, the inner sanctum of the Temple, reserved for the most sacred rites. This unique privilege allowed only once a year on Yom Kippur, underscores the gravity and solemnity of the day. The Day of Atonement is not symbolized by punishment, as some think, but by deep intimacy with a God who is willing to die for us.

Yom Kippur carries rich symbolism and meaning. It signifies the dwelling, atonement, and reconciliation of God and his people, mending the relational breaches caused by transgressions and sins. The elaborate rituals carried out by the high priest underscore not only the severity of sin and the desperate need for atonement but also how intimate the priest must become with God. These actions symbolize not only God's forgiveness for the sins of Israel but also highlight the nation's dependence on divine mercy through intimacy with it. This feast is asking those of us who are Christians a question: "We believe God forgave our sins and remained intimate with us, but are we also forgiving those who sin against us and remaining intimacy with them?" Don't just say "I forgive you," show it by inviting into friendship and intimacy.

While Yom Kippur is not traditionally observed in the Christian calendar, incorporating elements of its observance could enrich Christian spiritual practice. It could serve as a time of sincere repentance, introspection, and a renewed commitment to live in the light of God's mercy, as demonstrated through Christ's sacrificial act with people around us.

Yom Kippur also reminds us that Israel was chosen as God's people to be a witness not of their perfection but of a relationship between imperfect people and a perfect God (Isaiah 43:10-12). This calling, which is "irrevocable" (Romans 11:29), is meant to show that God loves and works through imperfect people. Much like any other relationship, the relationship between God and Israel includes ups and down."

In Jesus

To understand Yom Kippur's implications in the New Testament, one must delve deep into the symbolism woven into its rituals. Central to this day was the idea that sin requires atonement, a price to be paid. The repeated sacrifices of Yom Kippur, year after year, highlighted the insufficiency of animal sacrifices to permanently deal with humanity's sin (Hebrews 10:1-4).

Enter Jesus, who the New Testament proclaims as the Lamb of God. His sacrifice was not a temporary covering but a permanent solution, making obsolete the need for continual animal sacrifices. As the writer of Hebrews states, "But when Christ had offered for all time a single sacrifice for sins, he sat down at the right hand of God" (Hebrews 10:12). This one-time offering perfectly fulfilled and thus ended the sacrificial system set forth in the Old Testament.

By looking at Yom Kippur in the light of Christ's work, Christians can fathom the weight of their redemption. The day's solemnity underscores the gravity of sin and the monumental love God has shown through Christ's sacrifice. It reminds believers that atonement isn't a mere historical event but an ongoing reality, granting them access to God without barriers.

Moreover, the Day of Atonement was a day of communal reflection, fasting, and deep soul-searching. Just as Israel was called to examine their lives and turn from their sins, Christians are reminded to regularly assess their spiritual walk. Christ's sacrifice doesn't just offer atonement but also empowerment through the Holy Spirit to live righteously.

The narrative arc of the Bible, culminating in Jesus' sacrifice, underscores the intertwining of justice and mercy—God's holiness demanding atonement for sin, and His love providing it. As we journey onward to Sukkot, or the Feast of Tabernacles, we'll witness the grandeur of God's redemptive plan and the joyous celebration that stems from His saving acts.

The Feast of Tabernacles

(Sukkot)

Marking the culmination of the sacred cycle of Jewish festivals, the Feast of Tabernacles, known as Sukkot in Hebrew, brings the faithful into a time of reflection, rejoicing, and renewal. Commencing a mere five days after the solemn observances of Yom Kippur, Sukkot offers a contrast of joy and celebration, underpinning the diversity and depth of experiences encapsulated within the Jewish religious calendar.

The roots of Sukkot trace back to the book of Leviticus, where the children of Israel were instructed by God to dwell in temporary shelters, or 'sukkot', for a week. This ritual served as a poignant reminder of the Israelites' journey through the wilderness following their liberation from Egyptian bondage, a period marked by dependence on divine guidance and provision.

Sukkot, thus, stands as a commemoration of the faithfulness and protective care of God throughout the trials faced by the Israelites in their forty-year wilderness sojourn. It also coincides with the season of harvest, thereby making it an occasion for the Israelites to offer their gratitude to God for the bountiful yield. This element of the festival imbues it with an aura of joyous celebration, a time to acknowledge the blessings of the Almighty.

The relevance and significance of Sukkot extend beyond the confines of Judaism, offering profound insights for Christians as well. This festival can be viewed as a time for Christians to reflect upon God's faithfulness, mirroring the protection and sustenance God provided for the Israelites with His spiritual and physical provision in their own lives.

The New Testament provides accounts of Jesus celebrating the Feast of Tabernacles, further establishing the festival's significance within the Christian tradition. In one particularly memorable instance during Sukkot, Jesus declared Himself as the provider of 'living water', signifying His role as the source of spiritual nourishment and eternal life. This connection helps deepen the Christian understanding of Jesus, His teachings, and His divine mission.

Like many other Jewish festivals, Sukkot also carries with it the promise of future fulfillment. The prophet Zechariah prophesied a time when all nations will celebrate Sukkot in the Messianic Kingdom, indicating the universal embrace of this festival in the age to come. For Christians, this prophetic dimension of Sukkot instills a sense of eager anticipation and hope, reaffirming their faith in the ultimate realization of God's eternal promises.

In Jesus

In the time of Jesus, the Feast was marked with much rejoicing. One of the primary rituals involved the daily drawing of water from the Pool of Siloam, which was then poured on the altar in the Temple. This ritual, known as the Water-Drawing Ceremony, was a joyful oc-casion with music, dancing, and singing. The water symbolized God's provision during the desert sojourn and the hope for the coming rainy season. It also had Messianic implications, as it pointed towards a time when living water would flow from Jerusalem, quenching the world's spiritual thirst (Zechariah 14:8).

Against this backdrop, Jesus' proclamation in the Temple becomes even more potent. When He invites the thirsty to come to Him, He's not merely offering physical sustenance but eternal, spiritual nour-ishment. The "living water" He offers is the Holy Spirit, a constant wellspring that brings life, rejuvenation, and comfort to believers.

But Sukkot isn't just about remembering the past; it's also an antic-ipatory celebration. Jewish tradition holds that Sukkot foreshadows a future time of universal peace and divine fellowship, a time when all nations will make a pilgrimage to Jerusalem to worship God (Zechari-ah 14:16).

In the New Testament, this hopeful vision finds resonance in Je-sus' promise of the coming Kingdom of God. Revelations describe a future where God will "tabernacle" with humanity: "Behold, the tabernacle of God is among men, and He will dwell among them, and they shall be His people, and God Himself will be among them" (Revelation 21:3). Jesus, the Emmanuel or "God with us," inaugurates this divine presence, and Sukkot becomes a poignant reminder of God's promise to be ever-present with His people.

In embracing the symbolism and traditions of Sukkot, Jesus not only confirms His messianic role but also offers a renewed understanding of God's continued presence and provision. The Feast of Tabernacles serves as a beautiful bridge between Old and New Testament teachings, uniting believers in a shared hope for a future where all are invited to partake in the divine banquet, to dwell in the eternal Sukkah, and to drink from the ever-flowing rivers of living water.

Other Important Jewish Observances for Christians

(Moadim)

In addition to the seven biblically mandated feasts, there are other significant observances in the Jewish calendar that bear relevance to Christians. These festivals can deepen a Christian's understanding of the shared historical and spiritual roots between these two faith traditions.

Hanukkah: The Festival of Lights

Hanukkah, or the Festival of Lights, an eight-day festival typically falling in late November to late December, commemorates the rededication of the Second Temple in Jerusalem and the miracle of the oil that made the lamp's light last eight days. This festival is a poignant reminder of faith, resilience, and divine intervention, which resonate strongly in Jewish and Christian traditions. But most of all, of living in the light.

Although Hanukkah is not mentioned in the Old Testament, it is referenced in the New Testament, specifically in John 10:22-23. Here, we find Jesus in Jerusalem during the Festival of Lights, or Hanukkah, while preaching himself as the world's light (John 8:12). Understanding Hanukkah's historical and spiritual context can enhance a Christian's comprehension of this passage. Furthermore, the broader themes of light overcoming darkness are emblematic of Christian teachings, making Hanukkah a deeply symbolic observance for Christians to consider.

Purim: The Feast of Lots

Purim is a joyous festival that commemorates the deliverance of the Jewish people from a plot to destroy them, as recorded in the Book of Esther. This celebration serves as a reminder of God's hidden providence and the deliverance of His people, themes prevalent throughout the Bible.

Understanding the Feast of Lots can deepen a Christian's appreciation of God's sovereignty and providence for his children. The story of Esther, central to Purim, illustrates God's protective hand over His people, even in the face of imminent danger. This theme is echoed throughout the Bible and is foundational in Christian belief, reminding believers of God's unwavering protection and faithfulness.

Tisha B'Av: A Day of Mourning

Tisha B'Av is a solemn day of fasting and mourning that commemorates the destruction of both the First and Second Temples in Jerusalem. This day serves as a poignant reminder of loss, especially of God's presence and the hope for restoration.

For Christians, the themes of Tisha B'Av offer a deeper understand- ing of the significance of the Temple in Jerusalem and the promise of ultimate restoration through Christ in the New Jerusalem (Revelation 20-22). Both Jewish and Christian traditions anticipate a time of fu- ture redemption and restoration, and Tisha B'Av serves as a profound reminder of this shared hope. Understanding the significance of this observance can deepen a Christian's understanding of these themes and enhance their faith journey.

In summary, these Jewish festivals and observances offer Christians an opportunity to deepen their faith by exploring the shared historical and spiritual roots between these two traditions. By understanding and respecting these observances, Christians can further enrich their spiritual journey, appreciate the breadth and depth of God's engage- ment with His people, and foster a more profound connection with their faith's biblical origins.

The Sabbath

(Shabbat)

Among the numerous rituals and observances in Jewish tradition, the Sabbath, or Shabbat in Hebrew, holds a unique and central place. It is not an annual festival like the others we have explored, but a weekly observance, deeply woven into the fabric of Jewish life. It serves as a day of rest, worship, and family time, drawing its significance from the biblical Creation story and the Exodus narrative.

The Sabbath finds its roots in the earliest chapters of Genesis (2:2-3), where God Himself is depicted as resting on the seventh day after the work of Creation. The commandment to observe the Sabbath was then given to the Israelites in Exodus 20:8-11 as part of the Ten Commandments. They were instructed to set apart the seventh day of each week, doing no work, in remembrance of God's rest after creation and their own liberation from slavery in Egypt (Deuteronomy 5:15).

The Sabbath is rich in symbolic meaning. It signifies rest and cessation from labor, echoing God's own rest after the six days of creation. It also commemorates the Israelites' deliverance from slavery in Egypt, serving as a weekly reminder of their freedom and God's salvific actions.

Shabbat is more than a day of rest; it is a day to disconnect from the routine and pressures of everyday life and reconnect with God, family, and one's spiritual self. It's a day of joy and celebration, characterized by prayer, study of the Torah, and festive meals.

In Christian tradition, the concept of Sabbath has been transferred to Sunday, the first day of the week, in celebration of Christ's resurrection. However, the principles of rest and worship remain key elements of the Christian Sabbath. It is typically a day for communal worship, prayer, and reflection on the teachings of the Bible.

Understanding the Sabbath in its Jewish context can deepen Christians' understanding of the value of rest, the rhythm of work and worship, and the sacredness of time. It emphasizes that taking time for rest and worship is not simply a lifestyle choice, but a divine command and an integral part of human well-being. It also reminds us of our soul's eternal rest in Christ.

In Jesus

In the Ten Commandments, God commands His people to "Remember the Sabbath day, to keep it holy" (Exodus 20:8). The observance of the Sabbath was a sign of the covenant between God and the children of Israel, and it carried with it profound theological implications about God's character and His relationship with His creation. However, by the time of Jesus, the Sabbath had, for many, transformed into a burdensome day shackled by legalistic rules and regulations.

Yet, in the midst of these stringent interpretations, Jesus came with a refreshing perspective: "The Sabbath was made for man, not man for the Sabbath. So, the Son of Man is Lord even of the Sabbath" (Mark 2:27-28).

This declaration of Jesus brings to the forefront a vital truth. The Sabbath, in its purest essence, was not about legalistic observance but about holistic well-being – a time to rejuvenate, connect with God, and recognize our dependency on Him.

Jesus' interactions on the Sabbath, where He healed the sick and ministered to the needy, underscore this principle. By doing so, He was not breaking the Sabbath; instead, He was restoring it to its rightful place as a day of blessing, hope, and restoration.

More profound still is the realization that Jesus Himself embodies the true spirit of the Sabbath. In Matthew 11:28, Jesus extends an invitation: "Come to me, all you who are weary and burdened, and I will give you rest." This is not merely physical rest but a deep, spiritual rest that rejuvenates our souls. Through His life, death, and resurrection, Jesus has provided rest from the burdens of sin, brokenness, and the endless cycle of striving. He becomes our Sabbath rest.

For the believer, every day becomes an opportunity to enter into this Sabbath rest that Jesus offers. While the physical observance of a day of rest remains beneficial, the New Testament believer finds true rest not in a day but in a Person. As the author of Hebrews notes, "For anyone who enters God's rest also rests from their works, just as God did from his" (Hebrews 4:10). Jesus, as our High Priest, has made a way for us to continually dwell in this rest.

In today's fast-paced world, the message of the Sabbath is perhaps even more pertinent. It's a reminder that we're not defined by our productivity or accomplishments. Our worth is intrinsic, rooted in our identity as children of God. Jesus, as our Sabbath, beckons us to lay aside our burdens, to find a rhythm of grace, and to dwell in the peace that surpasses all understanding.

As we navigate the challenges of life, let's remember that our true rest is found not in a day but in Jesus. He is our Sabbath, our sanctuary, and our solace. In Him, we find the rest our souls so deeply crave.

In conclusion, while the Sabbath may not be a "festival" in the same sense as the others we have explored, it is arguably the most frequently observed and the most deeply embedded in Jewish and Christian religious life. Its lessons of rest, liberation, and the sacredness of time have timeless relevance and serve as a weekly reminder of our relationship with God.

Embracing Jewish Festivals as a Christian Community

As we round off our exploration of the Jewish festivals, it's essential to contemplate how these traditions, so deeply embedded in the fabric of Jewish religious and cultural life, can be acknowledged and celebrated within the context of Christian communities. The foundations of Christianity are intrinsically intertwined with Jewish history and religion. As such, participating in or understanding these festivals can serve to deepen Christian faith by reconnecting with its roots, enriching its practice, and enhancing the sense of fellowship within Christian communities.

Each Jewish festival offers unique insights into the Christian faith. Passover can remind Christians of Christ as the sacrificial lamb, while the Feast of Unleavened Bread invites introspection and spiritual purification akin to the Lenten period. The Festival of First Fruits can foster an appreciation for God's provisions, and Sukkot can serve as a time for communal celebration and gratitude for God's faithfulness. Simultaneously, these festivals provide a prophetic lens through which to view the life, death, resurrection, and return of Christ, thereby deepening the understanding of His role and mission.

In practical terms, Christian communities could choose to engage with these festivals in various ways. For instance, participating in a Seder meal during Passover or building a sukkah during the Feast of Tabernacles could be powerful communal activities that foster fellowship and deepen faith. Alternatively, communities might choose to commemorate these festivals through dedicated sermons, study sessions, or special prayers that emphasize the shared spiritual heritage and divine narrative that unites Christianity and Judaism.

However, it is crucial to approach these celebrations with respect and sensitivity. While these festivals provide an avenue for Christians to explore their faith's Jewish roots, they should not be seen through the "you must celebrate these festivals, or God will hate you!" legalistic approach.

In conclusion, understanding and engaging with Jewish festivals can open a treasure trove of spiritual enrichment for Christians, providing a historical, prophetic, and practical lens to explore their faith. It serves as a reminder of the common ground that Christianity shares with Judaism and the spiritual lineage that binds them together. This exploration of Jewish festivals is not just a study of ancient rituals, but a journey into the heart of Christian faith - a faith that was born in the cradle of Judaism, grew under its shadow, and continues to draw nourishment from its deep wells of wisdom.

This book has aimed to serve as a bridge of understanding, connecting Christians with their Jewish roots while also providing a resource for Jewish people to understand how these festivals point to Yeshua, our Messiah. I hope that in these pages, readers from both faiths have found mutual respect, learned from one another, and recognized the deep, intertwining roots of these two great religious traditions.

Ultimately, these festivals underline a shared faith in a God who delivers, provides, and keeps His promises - a God of liberation, sustenance, and eternal love. And it is this shared faith that holds the potential to unite, foster mutual respect, and nurture an environment where peace can flourish. Let us remember, as we draw this journey to a close, that our shared celebrations and histories can serve to bring us closer, fostering an environment of understanding and camaraderie that can only serve to enrich our spiritual journeys. May these insights bring you peace, joy, and a deeper connection to your faith.

I pray that this modest volume will serve as a bridge fostering mutual understanding. From a Christian perspective, I hope it inspires an appreciation for the deeply ingrained Jewish roots of the faith. From a Jewish perspective, my aspiration is for this work to be an evangelistic tool, shedding light on how the festivals, in fact, point to Yeshua, our Messiah. May this book encourage unity and conversation and deepen our collective understanding of these significant biblical feasts.

Lastly, I would like to ask for a favor: Please consider leaving a short review (or at least a rating) for the book on Amazon! I also invite you to check out my other books, available on the Amazon store.

Printed in Great Britain
by Amazon